A COLLATION OF WAR POEMS

Jean Marie Palmer was born in West Middlesex Hospital, Isleworth, in 1951 and lived in Twickenham until 1963. From there she moved to Hampton, Middlesex, where she still lives. Now enjoying her retirement, Jean has found more time for writing short stories and poems – a hobby she has always loved. In these poems Jean expresses her thoughts and feelings on the horrors and sorrows of war while paying tribute to the selflessness and courage of Britain's armed services in two world wars.

A COLLATION OF WAR POEMS

Jean Marie Palmer

ARTHUR H. STOCKWELL LTD
Torrs Park, Ilfracombe, Devon, EX34 8BA
Established 1898
www.ahstockwell.co.uk

British Library Cataloguing-in-Publication Data.
A catalogue record for this book is available
from the British Library.

ISBN 978-0-7223-4725-6
Printed in Great Britain by
Arthur H. Stockwell Ltd
Torrs Park   Ilfracombe
Devon EX34 8BA

1914–1918

So many years have gone by,
Since the start of World War One.
How many parents left to cry
When they lost their only son?

They fought to save dear England,
By God, they won the war.
They fought so hard, with guns in hand,
They saved our precious land.

Horrendous things they had seen,
No man should ever see.
But they fought for England,
And for the likes of you and me.

The war had lasted four long years,
With pride, we now recall.
Every year we honour them
At the Royal Albert Hall.

A Dream for the Future

When Tommy came home from the war,
He left his mates behind.
Was he one of the lucky ones?
For it left him only blind.

We have so much we owe them,
We never should forget.
No doubt there'll be another war,
Of that you sure can bet.

Wouldn't it be lovely
If we could live in peace,
And all the wars around the world
Would finally come to cease?

Until that day, we should pray,
That time will surely come.
Then all the forces round the world
Will live together, as one.

A Message for the Future

The war's been over ninety years,
But did the people learn?
I'd like to think that they did,
But the earth still tries to burn.

I hope they learn before too long,
Before it is too late.
They've got to know that war is wrong,
And banish all this hate.

So listen, all you heads of state,
You know peace must prevail.
And all the wars upon our earth
Must surely wear a veil.

Bells

The bells ring out at Christmas time,
Now the war has passed.
No one knew in '39
How long the war would last.

So many people lost their lives,
This sacrifice they made.
But we'll go on with our lives,
Ours that God has saved.

We'll live for them every day,
I thank those whom I had met.
We'll raise our glass at Christmas time,
We shall not forget.

Christmas Day, 1914

The guns of war fall silent,
They sleep on Christmas Day.
How so quiet is this day
I've longed for and I've prayed?

Please hide the blazing guns of death,
Bury them so deep.
The secret of their whereabouts
You must forever keep.

Christmas Eve, 1914

'Silent Night' is being sung,
Their voices sound so sweet.
But here we sit in this dung,
I wonder could we meet.

Our candles flicker in the wind,
This night is Christmas Eve.
Oh, dear Lord, have we sinned?
Our souls, would You receive?

Now we walk across this land,
The land we're fighting for.
Here we shake them by their hands.
How could we ask for more?

What would happen if we ran?
Then we could go home.
But we know that can't be done,
There is nowhere we can roam.

Exchanging gifts on Christmas Eve,
A football comes to light.
We kick the ball and have a game,
It's better than the fight.

I'm glad it's England we're here to save;
I'm glad I didn't run.
Will they say that we were brave
In the following years that come?

Back in our trenches, we all think
Those souls are just likc us.
As we sit here in this stink,
Our lives in God we trust.

Dawn

Dear Mother, I am writing
To you to say goodbye.
Please don't think so bad of me,
I'm on my way to die.

They say I am a coward,
I didn't want to fight.
They asked me why I ran away,
I was frightened of the sights.

They say I had deserted,
But I was full of fear.
God, I'm only human,
I love you, Mother dear.

One day the world will understand,
Cowards we were not.
They will rue this fateful day,
This day, when we were shot.

Daydream

Another year has just begun,
Let's pray for peace all round.
We'll do away with bombs and guns,
Image that peaceful sound.

Now listen, world, please take heed,
We're all fed up with crying.
Now, don't you think enough's enough?
There's been too much of dying.

So come on, all you nuts out there,
Open up your eyes.
Look above and you will see
A lovely bright blue sky.

Dear Mum

May I come home for Christmas?
I've been away too long.
Now I know, and understand,
That war is very wrong.

May I come home for Christmas?
I miss you so much, Mum.
How I long to see your face,
And feel the warming sun.

May I come home for Christmas
And sit in my favourite chair?
I know I lied about my age,
I wish I'd never dared.

Now the war has ended,
There'll be peace for evermore.
Please listen out, dear Mother,
For my knock upon our door.

Don't Weep for Me

Don't weep for me, dear Mother,
I'll make you proud of me.
I'm off to join the navy,
And fight the war at sea.

I know I'm young, but I'll soon learn
To beat the dreaded foe.
So, as I say, don't weep for me
When you see me go.

When I come back, I'll be a man,
I'll hold my head up high.
But if by chance I'll not return,
I'll see you from the sky.

Dream On

All the wars have ended,
Peace is here at last.
How we've waited for this time
We've prayed for in the past.

This should have happened years ago,
Think of all the cost.
Surely, it is worth it
When you think of those lives lost?

Then something wakes me from my sleep,
The rain outside is teeming.
Those lovely thoughts I will keep,
Till then I'll keep on dreaming.

Eighty Years On

I have seen the years go by,
My friends have all grown old.
Oh, how they have suffered,
As the eighty years unfold.

We thought it was 'to end all wars',
If that was only true.
Now, looking down upon the earth,
It seems they've not a clue.

As I look back to '39
I think, 'God, not again.'
But if it were all up to God,
No man would seem insane.

Now my friends are twisted up,
From the hard work they have done.
Me? I'm still a youngster,
For I fell in World War One.

Field of Poppies

The poppies stretch for miles and miles,
A massive sea of dark-red flowers.
Young lives lost, but not forgotten,
In those vile and darkest hours.

The poppies blow from side to side,
The sense of this we must not hide.
So many men lost their lives,
Many tears their wives had cried.

Mothers, sisters, mourn forever,
But carry on they must.
Just as the poppies in the field,
They shall never turn to dust.

Harry

One last look upon my grave,
My duty now is done.
English folk will not be slaves,
We will never run.

As I leave this troubled place,
I walk towards the light.
Just like others, I leave my trace,
And we'll always win the fight.

Home at Last

To see those cliffs of Dover,
To know you're home at last.
Away from mud and gunfire,
Away from fear and blasts.

We did a lot of crying,
We shed a lot of tears.
We lost a lot of lovely mates
Throughout those awful years.

Whilst lying in our trench at night,
We'd think of dear old Blighty.
The country that we dearly love,
The one that's great and mighty.

Now we're back on solid ground,
We've set dear England free.
Please, God, the fighting's ended,
To you, my Lord, I plea.

Home for Christmas

I've been away to Passchendaele,
To fight this wretched war.
Mother, please don't ask me
Of the haunting things I saw.

Mother, can't you hear me?
It's me, your darling Ray.
Mother, can't you see me?
I've come home on Christmas Day.

Why are you weeping, Mother?
There's nothing left to fear.
At last, I'm home to see you,
Please wipe away your tears.

As I look into the mirror,
There's no reflection there.
Yes, now I remember,
It was that awful flare.

I wish that you could hear me,
And all the words I say.
But just you wait and see next year,
I'll be home on Christmas Day.

I Didn't Want to Go to War

I want to stay in this trench
Until this war has passed.
I didn't want to go to war,
It wasn't me who asked.

How I want to be at home,
With my wife and my child.
I didn't want to go to war,
My manner is so mild.

How many other men are scared?
Maybe there's quite a few?
I didn't want to go to war,
I ask you, sir, did you?

Look Over Me

This trench has been our hellish home
For thirteen weeks or more.
How I want to run away,
But it's England I'm fighting for.

I hear that we are to advance,
Help me through this hell.
Please, let me see tomorrow,
For this story I must tell.

God, help me, give me courage,
We're to gain some precious land.
So I say to You, dear Lord,
Guide me by my hand.

Are You looking down on me
As I climb out of this trench?
If You are, my precious Lord,
I beg please give me strength.

Will I look back in future years
And recall this haunting scene?
But by then this muddy field,
Will again be rich and green.

Marching

Marching, marching, all day long,
My thoughts are of the past.
How many men have I killed?
How long will these thoughts last?

Marching, marching, my feet are tired,
Soon we'll have a rest.
All my friends that I had known
Truly were the best.

Marching, marching, nearly there,
I can see the port.
Will I again see my mates –
Those who have been caught?

Marching, marching, to the boat,
It's time to rest our feet.
Oh, the joy, what relief,
As I sit upon the seat.

The boat sets sail; we're on our way,
The past has been such hell.
I'll remember all my friends.
I'll remember where they fell.

My heart is feeling lighter
As we are leaving Rome.
For now the war is over,
And I am going home.

My Darling Son

My darling son, come back to me,
I know you died a hero.
Your duty's done, you died a man,
My love for them is zero.

Should I forgive? Maybe in time,
It's hard for me right now.
Maybe one day, I don't know,
But I ask the question, how?

Your name will live for evermore,
Just like those other men.
How I'll miss you, darling son,
You'll always be my Ben.

Don't worry for your little son,
I'll tell him of your life.
You died to help your country
That's living on a knife.

Maybe one day there will be peace –
We can only pray.
Until then we'll live in hope,
And wait for that miraculous day.

My Duty

Mother, please forgive me,
You know I had to go
To fight for king and country,
My death was such a blow.

I fought for king and country,
My heart knew where to go.
But I love you, Mother,
I had to fight our foe.

I know my body lies in France,
Beneath the deepened sod.
So I'll wait for you, dear Mum,
Until you meet our God.

1916

The day I stood on Platform 1,
I stood so neat, so proud.
I was off to fight for England,
Which was shrouded by a cloud.

As the train pulled into Dover
My heart was full of fear.
Will I again see England,
My country that's so dear?

When I reached the foreign shores,
There was fighting all around.
All I saw before me
Was death upon the ground.

How I've longed for England,
Have a stroll in Regent's Park.
But all I've known in this last year
Is living in the dark.

Two years have passed since landing here,
We've heard the war has ended.
But I can't help but shed a tear
For my mates, whose lives they've tendered.

Now the nightmare's over,
I'll throw away my guns.
For now I sail to England,
Back to my loving ones.

Over the Top

As day dawns I look around,
Letters are written, without a sound.
Fear in our eyes, but pride in our hearts,
We wait for the whistle, and then we'll start.

Letters were written to lovers and wives,
With love in our hearts, we tell them to thrive.
Our tears are dried up; it's time to be brave,
We as a nation will never be slaves.

The time has now come for us to line up,
With the last of the rum we'll have a good sup.
We'll all do our duties; we'll make them so proud,
We will get rid of that dirty black cloud.

Will I survive this day on the Somme?
Where is my brother, little wee Tom?
The officer raises his whistle to blow,
"Good luck, chaps, over we go."

Remembrance Day

We gather yet another year,
To remember those we've lost.
Now another war begins,
I ask you at what cost?

When will we learn the lesson?
When will we live in peace?
I beg of you, to all mankind,
Please, let the war now cease.

How many men will fall this time?
How many tears must flow?
I beg, please stop the killing,
But I know that you must go.

This earth is only lent to us,
We've made it such a state.
Soon it will obliterate
If we go on at this rate.

I for one don't want a war,
A coward, you might say?
But I want to see the children
Grow up one sunny day.

Run or Fight

If I had gone to war and fought,
The nearest hole I'm sure I'd sought
I'm not brave by any means,
I'm sure they'd call me Coward Jean.

But would I act in such a way?
I won't know until that day.
But I pray that day won't come,
Because these days I cannot run.

The Evacuee

I'm going to the seaside,
I'm going to see the sea.
But please, won't someone tell me
What is an evacuee?

All us kids are all lined up,
Our names are on our coats.
And when I see that lovely sea
I'll ride upon a boat.

I see my mummy crying,
She can hardly see.
But please, won't someone tell me
What is an evacuee?

Please come with me, dear Mummy,
Come and see the sea.
We'll have a lovely paddle,
So happy we will be.

Tonight I will be home, dear Mum,
Then you'll jump with glee.
But please, won't someone tell me
What is an evacuee?

The Lost Men of Burma

My father fought in World War Two,
In Burma and Ceylon.
But I know so many mates
Have sadly now passed on.

But my dad is still here,
He's nearly ninety-one.
He can rest in peaceful sleep
Now his duty's done.

I've never told him how I feel,
Maybe the time has come?
I'm so proud of you, dear Dad,
For the duty you had done.

Gordon Palmer
28/5/1921–1/5/2014
RIP

The Somme, 100 Years On

Today I think of those brave men,
A lot of them brave boys.
They picked up their deadly guns,
And put away their toys.

Did they know the slaughter
That would soon befall?
But they went to their deaths
When their duty called.

I thank them for my life today,
And our freedom now.
So, brave lads, I say to thee,
Today, I humbly bow.

Through the Eyes of a Soldier

Time slips by, my friends grow old,
Oh, what stories they have told.
We were told of hope and pride,
But in the end millions died.

How I fought for England,
How I tried my best.
But all it ever gave to me
Is eternal rest.

Training

"Left, right; left, right,"
That's all that I can hear.
The Sergeant's voice is so loud,
To his wife he is 'my dear'.

If she could hear him shout like this,
I'm sure she'd change her mind.
He's not so nice as she thinks,
And neither is he kind.

Another week of this old lark,
Then I'm overseas.
Then no more I'll hear his voice,
And he'll let me be.

A year has passed and I'm still here,
I thank that man so much.
He taught me more than I thought,
He really left his touch.

Under Age

Oh, my God, why did I lie?
They said it would be fun.
But here I lie, will I die
As I lie here in the sun?

But if I die, just like my mates,
We tried, it was our best.
So here I lie, is this my fate?
Here comes eternal rest.

England, oh, dear England,
I'll fight for you again.
Now God leads me by His hand,
I'm happy, no more pain.

VJ Day

VJ day came today,
Let's hope all wars have passed.
We don't want a troubled war,
Let's hope that peace will last.

We must have peace for all mankind,
Or are we really bloody blind?
We must not fight, we must survive,
That's if we're to stay alive.

But please remember those lives lost,
In wars that have gone by.
And don't be ashamed, when alone,
To have a little cry.

We Must Remember

Do I remember Tommy
And all those other men?
No, but I respect them,
For they gave their lives up then.

Oh, how brave they must have been,
Would I have run away?
But if my country needed me,
I would have had to stay.

But as it was, I wasn't there,
I wasn't even born.
But I respect their memory
Each and every dawn.

For my life I thank them,
I thank those who still remain.
We should learn a lesson
From their tears and all their pain.

Wear Your Poppy with Pride

Each year I wear my poppy,
My heart is full of pride.
My respect for those dear soldiers
I will never hide.

Those past and present men of war,
For me they stand so tall.
I'll wear my little poppy,
God bless them, one and all.

Who Were You?

I never knew your face, brave boy,
Your name I never knew.
But in my heart you won a place,
And there forever stay.

The things you saw, the things you did,
You know they had to be.
You had to fight for a better world,
I thank you for your deed.

You gave your life; you gave your all,
Your family sad, but proud.
I know not where you lie.
Maybe Westminster Abbey?